BY THE STREAM

MONTY HALE

BY THE STREAM

TATE PUBLISHING
AND ENTERPRISES, LLC

Published by Tate Publishing & Enterprises, LLC
127 E. Trade Center Terrace | Mustang, Oklahoma 73064 USA
1.888.361.9473 | www.tatepublishing.com

Tate Publishing is committed to excellence in the publishing industry. The company reflects the philosophy established by the founders, based on Psalm 68:11,
"The Lord gave the word and great was the company of those who published it."

Book design copyright © 2014 by Tate Publishing, LLC. All rights reserved.
Cover design by Rtor Maghuyop
Interior design by Jomar Ouano

Published in the United States of America

ISBN: 978-1-63185-981-6
1. Religion / Christian Ministry / Preaching
2. Religion / Christian Ministry / Pastoral Resources
14.06.18

To
Cindy
A Godly Wife
and
Mindy
A Chosen Daughter

In Memory
Bill R. Hale
1933-2014
A Godly Man
A Great Dad

Acknowledgements

The wealth of wisdom I've experienced from men like Dr. Carlisle Driggers, Executive Director Emeritus of the South Carolina Baptist Convention, Rev. John Moody, Rev. Russell Richardson, and Rev. Paul Wheelus, who were my childhood pastors, and my dad, Bill Hale, have greatly contributed to the writing of the book. My proof readers, Catherine Renfroe and Misti Ellis have been a wonderful blessing to me. Thank you also to Dr. David Parks, Associate Executive Director of the South Carolina Baptist Convention for challenging me to write this book. Finally thank you to my wonderful wife Cindy, daughter Mindy and my mom and dad who encouraged me to write a book that would hopefully encourage God's servants for years to come.

CONTENTS

THE TOUGHEST JOB
IN AMERICA

Leadership expert Peter Drucker once gave his opinion of the toughest jobs in America. He listed four not necessarily in order. The first was not a surprise; President of the United States. Neither was the second or third; hospital administrator and university president. But the fourth he mentioned was a surprise to most people— pastor of a local church. The plight of the local pastor has become almost unbearable. Most work endless weeks without any time off. When they are able to get away, either by themselves or with family, many are called back to their place of service because of a crisis. Stress related health issues are taking a toll on most pastors' physical, emotional, and spiritual health in unprecedented ways.

In fact, it is this author's opinion that being a pastor of a local church is the toughest job in America today. No other profession carries as dire consequences if derailment occurs. If a pastor experiences a moral failure, he not only loses his marriage and family, he will more than likely lose his profession and calling. That doesn't necessarily happen in the other *toughest jobs* that Drucker enumerated. If a pastor loses his health—be it mental, physical, or emotional—he will more than likely suffer shame and possibly not be able to continue to fulfill the call God has placed on his life. History is full of presidents that have failed morally, emotionally, physically, and even mentally and yet have fulfilled their terms of leadership. Not so for the pastor. Some have failed in these areas and have recovered, but the toll it took upon them and their families affected them for the remainder of their lives. So while you can argue that there are other tough jobs in our country, none carry the enormous consequences of failure as does the pastor of a local church.

That's what this book is about. In my work as a denominational leader, I talk to pastors and church leaders every day. Most of the time the conversations are not about how wonderful and easy the ministry is these days. My days are filled with coaching and encouraging

God's leaders to hang in there and hold on. To say the least, this constant bombardment of crisis takes its toll. Recently, I went through a physical breakdown of sorts caused by the stress of ministering to God's servants. The Lord literally put me on my back. I spent days looking up at the ceiling. In the midst of this tough time, I found myself praying like I never had before. I didn't pray so much for my healing as I did seeking the Lord for direction. My physical health betrayed me, but my spiritual health gained strength. Sometimes God has to do that to me. He has to completely knock me down before I will turn to Him.

One day, I found myself wrestling with a decision. God had placed me in an intersection and confronted me with a choice. Would I go straight ahead and continue along on this path, or would I once again surrender to Him? He would be with me no matter what I decided, but in my heart I knew he would confront me with this question at a later time. So stubborn and hurting, I surrendered. I turned a corner and proceeded on another path; the path of a deeper trust in the Lord. Yes, I've trusted Him for years, but this turn in the road was a steep incline. I knew it was going to demand things of me that I had rarely demanded of myself. This surrender was to take a path that would demand that I start driving the speed limit. That was not something I was used to. I knew some pastors that did. I labeled them as slow. I was more familiar with the blur of the world wising by my window. My life was about getting things done and making sure they were done in a way that I would not be embarrassed. You know, my way of doing things. The first few yards after the turn were crucial in this trusting journey. He showed me some things that I needed to pick up and some things that I could not take along with me. For instance, a critical spirit had overtaken me. I needed to be rid of that. So I'm doing my best to throw that out the window. I need the spirit of following, (not an easy thing for the first born of three brothers, all pastors).

My hope is that as you read this book you will see the world of ministry and being a pastor as it really is. I hope that you will slow down to the speed limit and look at your surroundings long enough so that you can realize that you have to quit trusting your ability and talent to get you through the day. I am praying that you will surrender with me to the path that leads straight up. You cannot take the things you have in your hands now. You have to take only those things that the Lord wants you to take. You have to realize that He is ahead of you blazing the trail. Some of you are dwelling in a desert and have been for most of your journey. There's more out there! A stream exists where life-giving water flows. It can give you renewed, healthy ministry.

So, evaluate your surroundings and make the choice. Let's go!

A BIBLICAL FOUNDATION
FOR MINISTERIAL HEALTH

That person will be like a bush in the wastelands; they will not see prosperity when it comes. They will dwell in the parched places of the desert, in a salt land where no one lives. But blessed is the man who trusts in the Lord, whose confidence is in him. He will be like a tree planted by the water that sends out its roots by the stream. It does not fear when heat comes; its leaves are always green. It has no worries in a year of drought and never fails to bear fruit

(Jeremiah 17:6–8).

Jeremiah lived during a time of change, political corruption, and spiritual drought. King after king during his ministry did evil in the sight of God. He warned of the coming judgment to no avail. His message was one of repentance. He pleaded with the people to turn back to God. He used several methods to get his point across. The Lord had him wear a linen belt that he later ruined symbolizing the ruined relationship between God and his people. He went to a potter's house and watched as a bowl he was crafting became misshapen. The potter had to start over shaping the bowl. The message to Israel was that they needed to endure the reshaping and remolding of the Father. The Lord instructed him to buy a field when it was evident that his prophesy of destruction was going to happen. Doing this symbolized that the Lord would restore his people once again.

He suffered persecution at the hands of his countrymen, which included physical persecution. Many of the officials of the time plotted his death and would have succeeded in killing him had the Lord not revealed the plot to him. Later in his life after proclaiming the word of God to a hard hearted, unwavering people, he lamented his life all together. Finally, the inevitable happened. Jerusalem was taken by the Babylonians which was led by King Nebuchadnezzar. Before it was totally destroyed, the temple was the scene of slaughter. Men, women and children were tortured and killed by the thousands. Those who were spared, the young men and women, were taken as slaves. We read about their brave stands for the things of God in the book of Daniel. Jeremiah was also spared. As the captives were being led off to Babylon, he tells them to settle in the land, plant a garden, have children and pray for its prosperity. They were going to be there for a while. He was right.

In the 17th chapter, he pleads with the people of God to turn back to following the ways of God. He declares that their sin is not written on an erasable scroll, it is engraved on a stone. It is literally set in stone. The destruction is inevitable, but there is hope. Surrender to the things of God! He compares the ones who trust in themselves with those who trust in the Lord. The difference is remarkable. They are two totally different species of plants in two totally different settings. One exists in the deadness of the desert; the other thrives by the stream.

These and other themes in this book speak to the journey that every pastor needs to consider. The choice is clear, stay in the desert or surrender and trust the Lord. It will mean that He will rip you up by the roots of your life and plant you near the stream. No matter, He will begin pouring his life-giving nutrients into you. After years of this transformation, your life and purpose will be renewed. You will become a new creation. Too many of us have decided to stay where we are and our physical, emotional and spiritual health is showing the wear. Without a clear surrender we endure the perils of desert thinking and living. When we live and think this way, we actually believe that this is what ministry is supposed to be. We have lived this way so long that we don't think there is any other way. Some of us even like the idea of hanging out in a desolate place. It requires little growth or effort and we know what's going to happen next, so we feel secure. Then there's the sick who actually think that unless they are suffering they are not really ministering. So, these stalwart crusaders spend most of their lives in victimized self pity, *suffering for Jesus*.

A couple of decades ago, I went on a mission trip with a group from the church where I was the pastor. We came from our small church in Kansas to do some construction and remodeling for a Native American congregation in Oklahoma. Some of the folks on the trip decided to work hard during the days but spend the nights in a nearby motel. I was one of those folks. I will never forget the reaction of one of our older members when she was given the option to stay at the motel, or camp out at the church. She said, "No way, if I went to a motel I wouldn't feel like I was on a mission trip!" Somehow she believed that if her surroundings were not austere then she was not being spiritual. It wasn't too many days before she became totally worn out and nearly too ill to continue with her ministry to the children of the church. It didn't take much cajoling to get her to surrender to the comfort of the air conditioned motel. After a full night of sleep and a great shower, she told me, "I guess I should have listened to you, preacher. I was trying to be more spiritual than my body could endure." Many of us are just like that, and we are paying a terrible toll as a result.

I'm not just talking about your physical surroundings. I'm talking about your heart and mind too. Many followers of Christ believe that unless the Lord chases you down and puts you in a choke hold, you should never be a pastor. We have glamorized the ministry of those who have spent most of their lives as successful businessmen and women. If they have made it big in some Fortune 500 companies making millions of dollars, then were wrestled out of that life into the desert of ministry, we put them on a pedestal.

"Look at all they gave up to be a pastor of a local church," we said.

"I want that guy to lead my church, he gave up the abundance of the stream for the heat and desolation of the desert," others remark.

"What courage it takes to be a successful person, and then live a life of austerity in ministry somewhere. Why, he's just like Moses; royalty one day, goat shepherd the next."

While that is a trend among us these days, that's not the desert or the stream I am thinking of. This desert is more of your own choosing. It has little to do with how large your ministry is or how small your church is. It has to do with the state of being you find yourself in. I believe we struggle between the desert and the stream constantly. As I read scripture, I become more and more aware that the desire of the Father is that we live by the stream. It's not just any stream, it's His stream. His stream supplies everything we need to be the pastor and person He desires us to be. His stream doesn't flow with money or houses or land or anything material, not that any of those things are evil in and of themselves. It comes from a source that is eternal. It flows with things that cannot be measured by earthly standards. This book is intended to help you find that stream and begin receiving from its life-giving water. You may desire that, but are wondering what the first step might be to begin this journey. "What will it take?" you might be asking.

It will take one thing; Surrender. For some, that's not a difficult challenge at this point in your journey. You've already lost everything and surrender is at your doorstep. For others, self sufficiency, talent, education, leadership skills and personality have supported you for most of your ministry and surrender will be very hard. Either way, surrender is the first step. The rest of the journey is all about putting one foot in front of the other. We will deal with that later. For now let's look at some of the characteristics of the lifestyle of the desert in contrast with the stream.

PART 1
A BUSH IN THE DESERT

I have made two trips to Israel in my lifetime. The first was in August of 1984. I don't know why we decided to go in the summer. It wasn't a great idea. Besides the culture shock and jet lag, our little group of pilgrims also had to endure the summer heat. It was most intense in the desert that surrounds the Dead Sea. We wandered around the area for a couple days. On both of those days, the temperature climbed to well over 110 degrees. One of the places we stopped was Qumran where the Dead Sea scrolls were discovered and the historical home of the small first century Jewish sect called the Essenes. As we approached the small visitor's center, I was taken by five or six small bushes with bright red flowers in full bloom. I'll never forget wondering how these bushes were enduring the scorching heat. I sure wasn't doing very well. On further investigation, I noticed that the gardener had placed a small irrigation tube around each plant. Water, from small holes in the tube, was trickling out on the ground at the base of each plant. Once inside the air conditioned building I asked how often the bushes had to be watered in order for them to stay alive. The attendant told me that the water never stops during the heat of the day. "If we were to turn off the water the small plants would wilt and die in a matter of hours," he said. The bushes were literally being kept alive by a constant supply of water.

In chapter 17, the prophet Jeremiah compares the one who trusts in himself as a bush in the wilderness. There is not much natural vegetation in the wilderness. What does exist is anything but picturesque. Most of it is grey, without many leaves, and serves little or no purpose outside providing shade for the few small creatures that live in the barren wasteland. Some have existed for decades but have reached their full maturity early in their life cycle. As pastors and leaders in the Kingdom of God, we find ourselves in a precarious situation. The prophet of old confronts us with the question, "Will we trust ourselves or will we trust the Lord?" This constant struggle has plagued the leaders of God's people for thousands of years. Have you ever thought about what goes on in the life of a bush in the wilderness? Let me share a few things and draw some conclusions from these passages.

THE HEAT OF ANGER

"A hot-tempered man stirs up dissension, but a patient man calms a quarrel."

Proverbs 15:18

As I mentioned earlier, the heat of the wilderness is, at times, completely intolerable. My brother is currently a pastor serving in the Phoenix area. While it is tolerable in the winter, temperatures in the valley around Phoenix can soar to above 115–120 degrees in the summer. If you have ever been to the area during the summer months you know what I mean. He tells me that during those months, the highway department works during the night, not only to avoid the traffic, but also to avoid the heat. It's a hot desolate city. We have become a society that spends most of our days in the comfort zone of 68–72 degrees. Our homes, offices, churches, shopping centers, entertainment venues, and automobiles are designed to keep us warm in the winter and cool in the summer. More and more, I hear people say in the summer months that they are increasingly having trouble tolerating the heat. While a bush in the desert can adapt to the heat, the growth of the bush is limited because of it.

This is also true of the pastor/leader. Our *heat* comes from anger. Statistics related to pastoral burnout are all over the map, but most report that upward to 75 percent of pastors are dealing with stress that leads to bewilderment, anguish, and anger. I speak to hundreds of pastors and church leaders every year and I am finding that more and more of them are dealing with unresolved anger. In most cases it doesn't seem to be an inferno, it's more like a slow burn. It's right under the surface. Some have adapted to it, but have limited their growth, as well as their ability to bear fruit or lead in an effective manner. As Jeremiah says, "They wouldn't know success if they saw it." (Paraphrased) They are too distracted with being angry to know if God is doing a work in their lives or the life of their church. They just go from one angry criticism to another. Because of this attitude, they sit idle, not able to proceed or go back. They are dead in the water. The motor is running, but the boat is in neutral.

Several years ago, I took my wife to Hawaii for a special anniversary. One of the first places we visited was the Kilauea volcano on the island of Kona. The last eruption of this active volcano was in 1983 and it hasn't stopped since. We were told that things were somewhat under control the day we visited, so we were able to drive around the rim and even get out of the car and walk up to the edge. As we did, the smell of sulfur was everywhere.

As we looked over the side into the huge crater, steam flowed from the vents. From the explanatory signs that were placed in the area we learned that lava was always building under the surface. The vents were evidence that lava was flowing.

As I reflect on that visit, I compare it to many pastors I know and speak with on a daily basis. Many of them are like that active volcano. Lava is flowing right below the surface of their lives. It won't be long before an eruption will occur and the result will be a destructive mess. Many tell me at the end of the conversation, "Well, thanks, I guess I just needed to vent." I want to reply, "Oh, that's why I smell sulfur!" Venting is evidence that lava is flowing. So instead of venting and stinking up the world around you, find the source of the anger and deal with it. Unresolved anger not only paralyzes you, it also causes you to act out in a desperate need for escape. That escape can include a multitude of activities that will destroy you and your ministry. Angry pastors wear people out, including themselves. No one who wants to maintain their sanity wants to stay angry.

Think with me about what the heat of anger can do to your life.

It Zaps You of Your Strength

That's because it is tough on your body. Medical and psychological research has shown that no matter how much you exercise or eat correctly, you are putting yourself at risk if you do not manage your anger. Anger causes a widespread negative effect on the body.

It is important to understand what happens to the body when one becomes angry. In a moment of anger, you may experience muscle tension, grinding of teeth, teeth clenching, ringing in the ears, flushing, higher blood pressure, chest pains, excessive sweating, chills, severe headaches or migraines. With chronic anger, people can also experience peptic ulcers, constipation, diarrhea, intestinal cramping, hiccups, chronic indigestion, heart attacks, strokes, kidney problems, obesity, and frequent colds. Medical experts have found the heart muscle is affected by anger, and anger can actually reduce the heart's ability to properly pump blood.

The results of prolonged anger can also harm the body's largest organ the skin. People who hold in their anger often have skin diseases such as rashes, hives, warts, eczema, and acne. Researchers have studied the relationship of anger and skin disorders and discovered that when a person resolves his anger, skin disorders dramatically improve.

One of the major effects anger has on the body is the release of chemicals and hormones, primarily adrenaline and non-adrenaline. The adrenaline hormones act on all organs that reach the sympathetic nervous system, stimulating the heart, dilating the coronary vessels, constricting blood vessels in the intestines, and shutting off digestion.

Suppressed anger can also have psychological effects, causing depression, eating disorders, addictions to drugs and alcohol, nightmares, insomnia, self-destructive behaviors, and can cause disruptions in the way a person relates to others.[1]

It Dries You Up

If you have ever experienced dehydration due to being in the heat too long, you know what I mean. Dehydration is a condition that can occur when the loss of body fluids, mostly water, exceeds the amount that is taken in. With dehydration, more water is moving out of individual cells than the amount of water that is taken in through drinking. Medically, dehydration usually means a person has lost enough fluid so that the body begins to lose its ability to function normally, and begins to produce symptoms related to the fluid loss.

People (and animals) lose water every day in the form of water vapor in the breath we exhale, and as water in our sweat, urine, and stool. Along with the water, small amounts of salts or electrolytes are also lost. Our bodies are constantly readjusting the balance between water (and salts or electrolytes) losses with fluid intake. When we lose too much water, our bodies may become out of balance or dehydrated. Most doctors divide dehydration into three stages:

1) Mild,

2) Moderate and

3) Severe.

Mild, and often even moderate, dehydration can be reversed or put back in balance by oral intake of fluids that contain electrolytes (or salts) that are lost during activity. If unrecognized and untreated, some instances of moderate and severe dehydration can lead to death.[2]

Those who have chronic unresolved anger, or for our purposes, those who live in the desert constantly need water. Like the small bushes I mentioned earlier, if the flow of water stops the plants will die quickly. The problem is those who live in the desert of self trust have very little or no access to water than those who trust in the Lord have. Therefore, when they become angry many will run to temporary oasis like meditation, bio feedback, excessive exercise, medication or just ignoring it. Like many watering holes, they will give temporary relief, but once the water source dries up, (and it will eventually) the desert dweller must look for more sources of refreshment.

Many pastors and church leaders are what I call *oasis seekers*. They know they are in the wilderness, but instead of doing the hard work it takes to get out of the situation or trust in the Lord to walk through it to the other side; they wander the desert looking for another oasis. This is particularly the case of the angry pastor who has no desire to surrender. I've watched many of these wanderers attend conferences looking for the next thing to soothe their anger. They read books and go to self help seminars. They take time off, go hunting, or play golf. Some are carried away into pornography and immorality. Some get in the pulpit and pour their anger upon their congregations. I remember the story of the little girl who was in church for the first time. She had not been in "big church" before and was not familiar with the pastor and what went on. She had trouble sitting still and being quiet as most four or five year olds do. During the sermon the pastor began in his usual bombastic style, got red in the face, stomped around and yelled a lot. In the middle of all that the little girl tugged on her daddy's sleeve and asked, "Daddy, who's that man?" "That's our Pastor," the man replied. A few minutes passed, and then once again she tugged on her daddy's sleeve. "What is it honey?" the man asked. With her bottom lip stuck out and tears welling in her eyes she asked, "Why is he mad at me?"

In Lamentations 4, Jeremiah describes a portion of what happened to the people of God when they were under siege. He describes the princes (or leaders) as having skin as black as soot and bones as dry as a stick. They had no food or water for days. Even those who enjoyed the best food in the Kingdom now were in the streets begging. This is true of the pastor who allows the heat of anger to dry out his life. He trusts his own way to get him through the places of his life and ministry where only God can sustain him. Many of them are wondering in places with no food or water to sustain them. They are the living dead, zombies as it were; trying their best to remain regal, yet all the while ate up with anger.

Look at some of the symptoms.

Dry, sticky mouth. Is your preaching what it used to be? Is it dry? Are you spending most Saturday nights on the internet looking for a sermon to preach on Sunday?

Sleepiness or tiredness. More and more pastors tell me they are drained. They have no energy to lead anymore. Many times as I'm coaching them I find that they are really angry at their staff or church leaders for not going the way they want them to go.

Thirst. How's your Bible Study going? We'll deal with this in the second half of this book.

Few or no tears when crying. No compassion. I am always taken by the compassion of our Lord. You are probably familiar with his times of weeping at the grave side of his friend Lazarus. He had compassion for the people of Jerusalem and expressed it as he sat on the mount overlooking the city. When you lose your compassion or ability to cry, your spirit is probably dry and unresolved anger might be the cause.

Dry skin. I've always been told it takes thick skin to be a pastor. I guess that's true, but when we are continually angry our "skin" becomes dry and less flexible.

Headache. There is nothing worse than an aching head. It's hard to treat because a headache could be anything from simple tension to a malignant brain tumor. In and of itself it probably will pass, but constant anger will make it persistent.

Dizziness or lightheadedness. The inability to stay focused or in the moment is a symptom that something is out of focus.

I hope for your sake, and for the sake of those around you, that you will address this part of desert wandering. I believe it to be the largest issue that pastors face in our culture today (That's why this chapter is first and longer than the rest). If you continue to harbor it you will never get out of the desert.

THE RATTLESNAKE OF FEAR

"I have given you authority to trample on snakes and scorpions and to overcome all the power of the enemy; nothing will harm you."

Luke 10:19

I have always had a fear of snakes. It doesn't matter if they are large or small; they create terror in my life. I am particularly afraid of rattlesnakes. I've encountered one or two in the wild, but I will do most anything to avoid being within a 50-mile radius of them.

When I was about ten, a man in our church went out to the Rattlesnake Round-Up in Western Oklahoma. Yes, there is such a thing as a rattle snake round up. He carried a toe-sack full of the venomous creatures back to his home in Oklahoma City. On a hot summer Wednesday evening he brought those monsters to our church so that our boy's group could see them. All my buddies thought it was the coolest thing in the world. They were talking it up and proclaiming that they couldn't wait to see his collection. He didn't bring them in the church, (we weren't the snake handling branch of Southern Baptists), but he did bring them to the parking lot. When our teacher announced that we could go out and see the *bag of poison*, my friends all went running out the door. I tried to act as brave as I could, walking behind the pack with my eyes wide open with anticipation. Out to the parking lot we went. The rattlesnake cowboy stood near his pickup with a hissing, rattling sack full of snakes by his side. He carefully untied the top of the sack. When he reached in with a stick that resembled a golf putter with a hook on the end, I panicked and looked for my nearest retreat. I thought I was going to wet my pants. With the appearance of the third and the fourth, I ran to the edge of the parking lot and then eased my way back into the church building looking through the glass door. No one saw my hasty retreat because of their fascination with the rattlers. As he began to ease them back into the sack, I eased my way back to the group. When our teacher announced it was time for us to go back to the class, I was the leader of the pack and the first in my chair in the room. No one had witnessed my terror. I acted like everyone else, excited that I had seen a group of creatures that could have killed me with a single bite. But fear had gripped me. That was just one time that I learned to show a brave face, suck it up and act like everyone else.

Fear is prominent among ministry leaders. The greatest fear is being fired or forced to leave. To many the fear of being rejected by a congregation that you love and have poured your life into is the greatest of all failures. I know pastors who compromise their values and their understanding of the Bible in order to keep a paycheck. Many others have been caught in the web of financial crisis. They would be destitute and homeless if they were to stand for Godliness and truth. So, they go along with the crowd. All the while they are trying to get along with a bag full of snakes.

Like many of the prophets, Ezekiel faced fear. Like Jeremiah and other prophets he faced the daunting task of speaking life and light into people that were rebellious.

In the second chapter of Ezekiel, God spoke to his servant and said.

> "Do not be afraid of them or their words. Do not be afraid, though briers and thorns are all around you and you live among scorpions. Do not be afraid of what they say or terrified by them, though they are a rebellious house."

(Ezek 2:6)

God encouraged the prophet not to be afraid four times in one verse! So, he must have been terrified.

But He doesn't stop at encouragement. In Chapter 3, He gives him what he needs to overcome his fear of those he has been called to speak to. It all has to do with the Word.

Devour the Word

Ezekiel was given a scroll and instructed to eat it. So, he ate it and it tasted like honey. I know that's sort of a weird metaphor, but here's what I believe God is saying in these verses: internalize the word of God, and make the word of God part of who you are.

In my high school cafeteria there was a poster that read "You are what you eat!" I know the idea they were trying to get across had to do with nutrition and eating the right things, but I always thought that was an unusual saying.

As I have pondered on that poster over the years I have found that saying to be very true. If you eat the wrong things you will end up sick and die young. We devour a lot of stuff in our lives. The messages of Hollywood invade our lives every day. I have found that in order to overcome my fear I must internalize, or devour, the Word of God. I've noticed this to be especially true when I am going through a time of brokenness. It is in those hours that I find myself hungry for a Word from God. It is also in those times that I spend time in the word. I have even found God speaking to me in the Minor Prophets. Though they speak a lot about destruction, they also make sure their reader knows that God always has a remnant that he will build upon. It is in those hours that the Word becomes a filling beyond my ability to find satisfaction.

Declare the Word

In verses four and following, Ezekiel is told to go and speak the word of God to the people. It is not enough to take the word in, it must be spoken. That is the purpose of taking in the word. I have noticed something about people in middle age; we love to eat! Most of my middle age friends talk about food even while they are eating. Most of the time when I or one my fellow 50 somethings find, a restaurant that is particularly to our liking, we are eager to share all about the culinary delights of the place. The same is true of the Word of God. Ezekiel said the word was like honey in his mouth. That means it was good. He could have kept that to himself, but he was commanded by God to go share it with the people.

Notice here that the Lord doesn't put the responsibility of their response on the prophet. He is told to go share it, and if they respond that's fine, but if they don't it's not on him. It's not really about him anyway. It's not his Word he is speaking; it is God's Word he is speaking.

So many times we preachers think that if people don't respond we have failed. If you feel that way, it's because you have forgotten that it's not your word you must speak, it is God's Word. If they don't respond, that's on them not on you. Early in my ministry I felt that way. Then I heard Adrian Rogers, one of my heroes, tell the story of being in a revival at a church where night after night no one responded. Dejected, Dr. Rogers fell on his knees on the front pew asking why no one had responded to the word. That's when he turned to his scripture and realized it was not his responsibility to get people to respond, it was his responsibility to declare the Word.

If you have devoured His Word, it is your responsibility to declare it to the people God has given you. Don't be afraid, God's got this!

Be Hardheaded About the Word.

God acknowledges that the house of Israel has become unyielding and hardened toward His Word. In verse nine He tells the prophet of a change that will happen to him. God himself will make Ezekiel's forehead like the hardest stone, harder than flint. Then God encourages him again to not be afraid.

I know a lot of hardheaded people. They are stubborn, obstinate and downright mule-headed folks that won't be talked out of their position. They have the attitude of "Don't confuse me with the facts, my mind is made up!" You don't hear about many church folks these days that are hard headed about the things of God or His Word. If they are, they are labeled radical, extremist or some other title. Well, unless you ask God to make your forehead like a stone for His Word, you will never overcome your fear.

Please understand, I'm not asserting that you should grasp a piece of God's Word and hold on to it as if you can possess it. No, you cannot possess the Word of God by making it your opinion or your position. The Word is the Word. It's not about you or your position in life or your age or anything else that defines your identity. It's about what God says. As we are being used by God to deliver His Word, we come out of ourselves and our natural state of being and He forms us into who He desires us to be.

Overcoming your fear will require change. Sometimes God will break you. Other times, as in the case of Ezekiel; he will harden you. No matter, He will do whatever it takes to get his Word to His people.

So, call me a hardhead if you must. His Word leaves no room for debate. It is here that we all must stand in order to overcome our fear. Whatever you are afraid of, it will continue to leave you in the desert. Hear the gentle voice of the Lord encouraging you;

> "Do not be afraid of what they say or terrified by them, though they are a rebellious house."

> (Ezekiel 2:6b)

THE DROUGHT OF WORRY

"An anxious heart weights a man down, but a kind word cheers him up."

(Proverbs 12:25)

On most days here's how conversations go in my office.

"So, how can I help you today?"

"Well it's not something that I can put my finger on. I guess it's a concern more than an actuality."

Everyone has anxiety. We are all *concerned* about things in our lives. Many times those concerns get balled up and become anxieties. Those anxieties begin to roll on down the hill gathering other anxieties along the way. After years and years of this, a boulder sized snow ball of worry has over taken our lives and is destroying everything in its path. We worry about so much and it becomes such a habit that we borrow others worries just to feed our habit. After we have picked up all the snow of concerns and anxieties there's simply nothing left to pick up and we are in the desert.

Have you worried yourself into a drought? The desert is a place of dryness. Many people try to make the blistering heat of the desert more tolerable by reasoning that it's a *dry heat*. Some bushes survive in a drought. Some have adapted to living with little or no water, because they have to. You may have excused yourself from anything lush or green or abundant because you have adjusted to the drought of worry. It's become a way of life. So, you've learned to accept it, after all it's a *dry heat*. It's a dry heat that burns up everything that it bears down upon, except the most barren of all bushes and vegetation.

When I lived in Newton, Kansas we experienced a drought. It was nothing like the dust bowl days, but an extended drought nonetheless. As in Oklahoma, the wind blew relentlessly. The heat of the plains took control of everything. Everything that was green shriveled including grass, crops, and even trees. The entire world we lived in was brown. One of the things I remember most about those years was the large cracks that formed in the black clay of the area. I did my best to keep some of the trees and bushes around the parsonage alive. I gave up on the grass thinking it would come back once the moisture returned. We lost bushes and trees. The worst part of this dry time was that there was little hope for any renewal. The rain finally returned, but not after the damage of the drought was done.

Worry is much like those days in Kansas. It sucks the life out of everything that lives in your life. It also leads to other ailments and problems in the life of the pastor. The biggest worry among pastors these days is the fear of being terminated. The problem with this worry is that it causes a drought that might well lead to a forced resignation or termination. I will share later on how to keep yourself vibrant and full of life in ministry, but suffice it to say that worry will dry you up.

Winston Churchill said, "When I look back on all these worries, I remember the story of the old man who said on his deathbed that he had had a lot of trouble in his life, most of which had never happened." His words ring true in today's pastorate. One pastor wrote, "Most of our problems are huge, and they don't exist."

I wish I could say that I have learned to overcome worry. I have not. I have, however, found some spiritual disciplines to assist me when I worry. Let me share them with you.

Grace. Both God's grace and my grace. I have found that when I worry I have a need for God's grace. That comes from a life lived in brokenness. Restoration comes to the worried heart when God's grace comes in with its warming love and reconciliation. I too need to express grace to myself. Most of my worries are about my pride. It's amazing how I can make a situation that is totally not about me into something that totally is. It's almost as if I gather worry toward myself and hold on to it.

How sick is that? That's when I need to give myself the grace to realize it's not about me.

Rest. I worry most when I'm tired. Worry becomes emotional for me and therefore it exhausts me. That emotional tiredness wreaks havoc on my well being. Instead of waiting until you fall in the ditch, schedule times of rest. What do you do to recharge your batteries? Do it regularly.

Praise. Not necessarily singing. Praising the Lord and recounting how He has provided for you will conquer worry. Instead of focusing on the problem, focus on the provision. I am astonished how people have overcome the most devastating losses with the attitude of what's been given instead of what's been taken away.

Stillness. Those of you with ADD will not like this one. Somewhere we have learned that if we go harder and faster we won't have time to worry. We want to run from this drought instead of allowing the Lord to bring His life-giving rain in the stillness of our hearts. So we fill our lives with activities. We get up in the morning and we run until we fall exhausted in our beds at night. It may be raining, but we're going so fast we don't really notice or, even worse, we think it's a nuisance. Two words—Slow Down!

Silence. Not quietness, silence. Say nothing. Turn off everything and listen. In the silence you will hear Him and your worries will melt, as he says, "I am."

In June of 2012, my wife and I took a summer retreat to the mountains of Colorado. The place was lovely, the food was plentiful and the Holy Spirit was present. On the first afternoon we unplugged everything. No cell phones, no computers, no noise. As we sat there in shock listening to the silence, we heard the wind rushing through the pines and the gentle sound of the wind chimes that had been hung on the patio outside our room. It was if I heard the voice of Father saying, "All is well my child, take heart for I have overcome the world." The rest of the week was a great encounter with God. The teaching and outpouring of love was wonderful. We received the life giving charge that we so needed. However nothing compared to the daily time of sitting on the porch listening to the silence.

So, if you're worried, you're normal. If you've hung out in worry for some time you probably feel dry and parched. There's a way out. Stand still and wait. Wait for the rain to come. You can't control it. It comes from the Father himself. He's willing. Are you?

THE WIND OF CONTROL

"Submit yourselves, then, to God. Resist the devil, and he will flee from you."

(James 4:7)

I spent most of my life on the plains of Oklahoma. If you've been there you know that the wind blows all the time. In fact the first verse of the state song declares, "Oklahoma, where the wind comes sweeping up the plain…" I always joke that one day the wind didn't blow in Oklahoma and every one fell over. The trees actually grow toward the north, because of the relentless wind from the South. So, I'm familiar with wind and the havoc it causes. A cold day is frigid when it's windy. A hot day is hotter when the hot wind causes the environment to feel like a blast furnace.

That's what the wind is like for a bush in the wilderness. It makes a very harsh environment even less tolerable. The wind in the desert dwelling pastor is control. The number one reason why pastors are terminated or forced to leave Southern Baptist Churches has to do with the control issue. More specifically, the issue is conflict over who will be in control of the church. Many of these churches are dominated by a patriarchal system that has roots in one family that has intermarried within the church. In these cases a pastor is viewed as a chaplain that will be in the church for a time then move on to another place of service. Barna research states, a typical pastor has the greatest ministry impact during years five through fourteen of his pastorate. Unfortunately, the average pastor only lasts five years at a church. Many short pastorates occur when a pastor begins to be effective and control begins to shift from the patriarch/matriarch to him. That is usually when whispers in the hallway and the coffee shop turn to secret meetings and gathering of the troops. In short time the unsuspecting pastor is cornered and asked to resign. If he will not resign on his own, the group will attack his spouse and then his children until his spirit is broken and the wind of control sweeps him away. An estimated 85 percent of these men will leave the ministry and some will stop attending church all together.

Just as the wind blows from many different directions, the wind of control blows not only from the direction of the church, but it also blows from the direction of the pastor. A growing number of pastors have adopted the CEO leadership model in the church. While the model works well in the corporate system it causes conflict in the church system. The church system of most North American churches is a family system.

The smaller the church the more it is like a family. Most of the churches in North America are less than one hundred in attendance and tend to be dominated by one or two strong patriarchs. When a pastor who believes the church should be run like a corporation with him as the CEO comes into this tightly knit family system, conflict is inevitable.

Let me share a few observations about wind.

Wind is powerful. It is destructive. Understanding its power is the key to understanding how it works.

It is beyond your control. There was only one person who lived on earth who stilled the wind at His command, and he wasn't you.

It can be used for your good, if you know how to harness it.

John Maxwell tells a famous story about a man in his first church named Claude. You've probably heard how he began to understand how the wind of control was blowing through his little congregation. Claude was the patriarch and solidly in charge of everything in the church. Pastors had come and went and found themselves frustrated and damaged by the man that ruled the little kingdom. Maxwell found that if he would go out to the farm where Claude was working in the field or the barn and harness the wind of control, he could get much more accomplished than if he fought against it. He would go out there and talk to Claude about his dreams and vision for the church. He would ask his opinion before the board meetings. When the meeting came, Claude would stand and introduce the ideas to the rest of the board. More was done in that little congregation in those years than had been done in decades previously.

So who was in control? You may be thinking Claude was, but the truth was it was a shared control. Pastor Maxwell had the vision given to him by the Lord. He also had some ideas on how that could be accomplished. Instead of demanding his ideas and vision be adopted simply because he was the pastor, he went to this trusted leader and shared his ideas then listened and waited. He found in those years that Claude was the catalyst that could make those ideas happen. He also learned that leadership is not about doing everything. Instead, it's about influencing the people of God to get on God's agenda. We need to learn how the winds of control are blowing in our churches and harness that wind.

If that is going to happen, you must come to a couple of realizations. First, you must put down your need to get credit for every accomplishment in your church. Great leaders realize that they are nothing without those around them. Too many pastors are so hungry for control that they have to do everything in their congregations and therefore must do everything by themselves. Insecurity will make you desire credit for everything that is done in your church. You have limits. You can only accomplish so much. If you always want people to give you homage and chant your name, you will ultimately accomplish little and find yourself on the border of ineffective ministry. You have to have an attitude of who cares who gets the credit so long as God's will is being accomplished.

Second, recognize the brilliance of the group. There might actually be someone in your church that has a better idea of how to accomplish a given task than you do. We pastors get in deep weeds when we think we are the only ones that know anything about the vision or purpose for our church. That's just dysfunctional. When we think that no one has any good ideas except us, we are doomed to sail the boat of mediocrity. I read of a Christian organization that refers to the director's office as the place where great ideas go to die. The director is an insecure leader. As a result when his colleagues or those working for him present a new idea, he is so insecure that he just sits on the idea. He is in the paralysis of analysis. The organization hasn't moved in years and is nearing its own death because the leader believes that all the leadership is his. If it ain't his idea, it ain't a good idea. Please don't approach your ministry with the thought that you are irreplaceable. God's under control.

So, harness the wind of control and use its power to propel you effortlessly forward. Choosing to stand against it or even walk against it will erode your life. You will find yourself worn down and a shadow of your previous self. You didn't die for the world. Only Jesus could do that. So, get down off that high horse and serve the Lord. In serving Him, you will find a Master that loves you and is under control.

My tendency is to rush ahead and get to the location long before everyone else. In my younger years I hated the journey, always choosing to go the shortest route. I even saw traffic as a competition. I had to get ahead of the guy that just sped by me, so I would aggressively speed up and get by him to my exit. I wasn't going to let anyone beat me! In most cases I would *win*. Not many would beat me, but I found myself being beat. By that I mean I thought I was winning but I wasn't. As I look back on those years I find myself at a loss as to what I was trying to accomplish. In these last few years I found that winning means enjoying the Lord and serving Him. Then and only then do I know that He is God and I am not. Then and only then do I know that He's got this and I don't. That's when the wind of his Spirit begins to blow me out of the desert and toward His life-giving stream.

THE FREEZING NIGHT OF CONFLICT

"Without wood a fire goes out; without a gossip a quarrel dies down."

(Proverbs 26:20)

Although the desert is very hot during the daytime hours, it can get very cold when the sun sets. You may be familiar with stories of people lost in the desert who ended up freezing to death during the night. It's tough to imagine how it could get so cold that someone could literally freeze to death in an environment where it is so hot and windy that only the most adapted of vegetation and wild life could exist, but it is true. Temperatures vary greatly between night and day in many desert regions. Typically, humidity blocks the sun's radiation. Since deserts have little to no humidity, about twice the radiation is absorbed. At night, a greater amount of heat is lost due to the lack of humidity. This can bring temperatures well below freezing, especially during the winter months.

In a 2002 survey, two thirds of pastors reported that their congregation experienced a conflict during the past two years; more than 20 percent of those were significant enough that members left the congregation. Furthermore 40 percent reported a serious conflict with a parishioner at least once per month. But 31 percent indicated that conflict management was lacking from their seminary or Bible school training. Every church has conflict. Well most every church. If your church has no conflict, it's probably dead. So, conflict is inevitable in most churches. Jesus said, "In this life you will have trouble, (conflict) but take heart for I have overcome the world." Jesus guaranteed that we will have conflict in this world. He has overcome the world where the conflict exists. So, conflict is neither good nor bad, the important part is how you manage it.

Poor conflict management leads churches through a cold dark time. All of us know a church we would nickname the *Frozen Chosen*. Many times the church loses its power because conflict zaps all the strength of the members. Instead of concentrating on the needs of the community or those who need salvation in and out of the fellowship, the church spends all its collective energy battling the coldness that is brought about by mismanaged conflict. Without proper equipment and training, some in the church become frozen in their Christian walk through continuing conflict. As I mentioned before, conflict in church is made worse by the family system. When that system is an actual physical family, the dysfunction and hurt of that family comes into play in the church. That causes the conflict to become personal. That's why many churches are limping around in the Kingdom.

More and more churches believe that changing the leadership is the answer to their mismanagement ills. If things don't go well or if families within the church begin fighting or feuding, most of the time the pastor becomes the scapegoat. In a recent survey the editors of Christianity Today concluded that one out of four pastors say they have been forced out of a church due to personal attacks and criticism from small congregational factions. Duke's National Congregation Study says 9 percent of churches have had a conflict in the past two years that prompted a pastor or leader to leave-a number that seems to have held steady over time. In many cases this happens for decades and the church exists in the freezing cold night of the desert, trusting in itself and not the Lord.

Part of this mismanagement comes from our culture (especially Southern culture), and our refusal to confront potential conflicts. Before we know it, small issues become huge. Then a confrontation occurs. The point of ignition many times comes without warning and usually has little to do with the real issue. Many pastors tell me they didn't really see it coming. Many times that's because they have gotten used to living with the mismanaged conflict. They have put on enough layers that the cold has become tolerable and in some cases normal. Sure it's cold and in some cases an unbearable world, but hey it's our world. That attitude demands that the church continues to proceed without any effectiveness. The bad thing is that when the explosion is over and those on the side lines are in the process of picking up the pieces, those who caused the blow up are already gathering destructive materials to create another bomb.

In the South Carolina Baptist Convention nearly five hundred pastors and staff have been reported to have been terminated in the last seven years. We estimate that an additional 20 percent go unreported. While our convention has over 2100 affiliated churches, that number is still staggering. Nine of the top ten reasons for these terminations have to do with mismanaged people skills. Where there are people there will be conflict. So, 90 percent of the reason that pastors in our convention are terminated is because the pastor is not effectively managing conflict.

More and more pastors and staff members are finding themselves in a cold fellowship that refuses to confront the problems that cause these freezing nights. Many of the leaders have stopped confronting these things also because of fear of reprisals. Let me remind you that as a leader it is your job to have the hard conversations. If you refuse to do this, you will be the one that will bear the brunt of the storm.

When the Apostle Paul had a conflict with a brother, he dealt with it. The John Mark incident is a perfect example of how to deal with conflict in the church. On the first missionary journey John Mark came along, but midway through turned back home. At the beginning of the second journey Barnabas the great encourager wanted him to go with them again. Paul refused. He had no room for a person who had turned back when things got tough. So, Barnabas and John Mark went their way and Paul and Silas went another. Conflict everywhere, but conflict solved. Because of what seemed to be a terrible split, two groups of two were out sharing the Gospel instead of only one. Eventually Paul asks for John Mark to join him and so we see that though there were disagreements, when solved in a timely manner and with the leadership of the Holy Spirit, conflict turns out for good.

Please note these three things.

Dealt with in a timely manner. When is the right time to deal with conflict? Don Knott's famous character Barney Fife has a quote that is very appropriate. "You gotta nip it in the bud, Andy; nip it in the bud…" When you see that conflict taking shape, get to it quick and lovingly nip it.

The leadership of the Holy Spirit. Too many of us rush in where angels fear to tread. We don't wait on God's timing. Holy discernment is not too abundant among pastors these days. You must stay close to the Lord to know His ways and his thoughts. You must spend extraordinary time in prayer asking for discernment in dealing with these matters.

Leave the rest to God. Once it is settled, it is settled. Don't run after those who may or may not be offended. Let it be. More times than not God will use it and you will be able to move forward. It's His Kingdom.

THE SANDSTORM OF A CRISIS

"Do not let your hearts be troubled. Trust in God; trust also in me."

John 14:1

A meltdown is occurring in the Evangelical church in North America. While Christianity is expanding in unprecedented ways around the world, the North American Evangelical church is in a downward spiral of decline. In South Carolina we estimate that 20 percent of the population is in church on a given Sunday. Our state has over 5800 faith congregations of one brand or another. With a population of nearly four million, the church is virtually ignored. The leaders of these congregations become bewildered at what to do in a world inundated with churches, yet very few people attending them. It is a crisis that has not been experienced in the last two hundred years.

On my second journey to Israel, our group of pilgrims experienced something I had only heard about or read about, a sandstorm. We arrived on a cloudless beautiful day. When we awoke the next morning the sky was filled with sand brought there by the relentless South wind. The world was nothing like we had experienced or seen the last day. It had changed enormously. The sky was a brownish-red. Everything was covered with gritty sand blown in from the desert. Our excited group of travelers who were once excited about the places they would see on the journey were quickly discouraged and weary. The relentless wind and grit quickly took its toll on our group. The mini bus we were traveling in became filled with dirt. The air filters were clogged and before we knew it, we broke down. There we were, a once excited hopeful group seven thousand miles from home wanting to experience the Bible now we were completely discouraged and some even mentioned going back. We were a group in crisis. All the preparation for the trip, the money spent, the recruiting, the prayer of preparation, the travel out of the familiar, and we were quickly fading into discouragement.

I'm sure you know what I am talking about. You've prepared your life to lead the congregation that God has called you to. You've prayed; moved your family from a comfortable familiar place near family and friends, now a sandstorm of crisis has overcome your life. How in the world will you overcome such a sandstorm? Why would God lead me to this place only for a disaster to happen like this? What must He be thinking? Will there ever be a time when I don't have the grit of these insignificant problems in my life? We've all faced it. Maybe you're facing it now.

Let me share a few things about sandstorms and how to deal with the inevitable crisis they cause.

They are a natural occurrence in the arid climate of the desert. While we were panicking in the midst of the storm, the residents were going about their day. I asked our guide what to expect with the storm. His reply, "These things happen."

Some are worse than others. Take your queue as to their severity from those around you. It may be that all you see in the storm is dust and wind. You may think that the end of the world is at hand, but if you look around you and get the bigger picture it will in all likelihood calm you down.

Sandstorms pass. They don't last forever. Our tendency in the midst of a crisis is to think that the crisis will ultimately be the new normal. We think that this is the way the world is and there is no going back. I have to be honest that I thought that our trip was doomed. I wondered if I would ever recover from bringing this group half way around the world to endure a sandstorm the entire trip. Our driver sensed my panic latter in the day, put his hand on my shoulder and in broken English said, "It will pass." It did the next day. We endured the storm, and it clouded our experience at some of the sites, but it passed. The next day was bright and sunny again, and we went on to have a wonderful trip. As I look back on the experience, the storm added adventure and character to the journey. It gave us all a shared experience that we looked back on with a *we-made-it attitude*. We experienced other weather events while we were there, (It snowed one morning in Jerusalem), but the sandstorm proved to be the event that propelled us forward. It made the trip better.

So, what should you do if you're experiencing an event like this in your life? If you're in the midst of a storm, don't panic. Everything may look bleak, but it will pass and you'll be better as a result. Take a look at the big picture. This crisis and those to come will prove to be some of the greatest times of your ministry if you'll endure. Then, you need to ask yourself a couple of very important questions.

Do you want to stay in a place where they happen all the time?

Do you want to live your life going from one crisis to another?

Many leaders do. They wouldn't know how to survive unless they were dealing with a sandstorm. Still other leaders create sandstorms. Somehow they enjoy the turmoil. It's a way of life. But it is not the way of God.

In the desert sandstorms are inevitable. What you do when you're in the middle of one will determine your ability to lead on the days when the storm is not raging around you.

A bush in the wilderness endures and waits. It adapts and does the best it can to survive. It has the attitude: *That's just life. There is no other way. I'm a bush and this is the way I live. I trust in myself. The things I know are the things that are around me.* If you've thought or said anything like that, you've probably decided to live in the desert.

Unlike the bush, we have a choice. Jeremiah says that the one who trusts in the Lord has a new place of residence. You don't have to pull up your roots and tumble down the road to this place, but you must change the source of your life. It comes from trusting the One who is the life giver. From His heart flows a life giving stream that is much different from the desert that surrounds it. This is the choice that faces every leader and every follower of the most-high God. So, what's it like to live by the steam?

PART 2
A TREE PLANTED
BY THE STREAM: YOU ARE
A UNIQUELY CREATED BEING

"For you created my inmost being; you knit me together in my mother's womb. I praise you because I am fearfully and wonderfully made; your works are wonderful, I know that full well."

Psalm 139:13–14

"Peter turned and saw the disciple whom Jesus loved was following them. When Peter saw him, he asked, 'Lord what about him?' Jesus answered, 'If I want him to remain alive until I return, what is that to you? You must follow me.'"

John 21: 20–22

Every person who has lived or is living on this planet is a unique creation. We are all created in the image of God, but not one of us is completely like the other. Each of us have been wired and gifted uniquely. Even identical twins who share much of the same physical, mental and emotional characteristics are still uniquely made. There are an infinite number of ways that God has at His disposal to wire up and gift people. You are just one example of His wonderful creation. (Psalm 139)

If you like puzzles, you have probably found the Rubik's Cube. Invented by Hungarian sculptor and Professor Erno Rubik in 1974, the 3-D puzzle was originally called Magic Cube. Many people find the puzzle intriguing; others find it frustrating! Someone has figured out that there are over 40 *trillion* ways to set up Rubik's Cube. That's trillion with a t. While that may sound like an infinitesimal amount, it pales in comparison to the created order. You are in the midst of all that diversity. You are God's uniquely crafted beloved child.

As a Uniquely Created Being, You Have One Goal

The Apostle Paul wrote to the Philippians:

But whatever was to my profit I now consider loss for the sake of Christ. What is more, I consider everything a loss compared to the surpassing greatness of knowing Christ Jesus my Lord, for whose sake I lost all things. I consider them rubbish that I may gain Christ and be found in him…

Philippians 3:7–9a

As he was being formed into the image of Christ, he left those things that were of no value to his spiritual formation. He threw them on the trash heap and came to understand that the most important thing in life is knowing Christ and being known by Him.

It may be that while you have been involved in the work of ministry, you have left the way of the Lord and wandered on to some side streets, leaving your unique individuality stuffed away in a long forgotten corner. The life of ministry, like Rubik's cube, can have many faces and many trials that are challenging and seemingly insurmountable. Sometimes we can even lose our spiritual edge, or forfeit our family or ministry.

In my years of working with pastors ranging from those early in ministry to those who have decades of ministerial experience, I have found two common threads that woven together, have diverted us from the goal of knowing and being known by Christ.

We have lost sight of our unique image and individuality in Christ.

We have stopped striving toward this ultimate goal. We've gotten caught up in the doing of ministry and left being in ministry behind.

Because of this…

- Many of us have wandered off into things that should have been thrown on the trash heap. Some of those things are good things, but not the most important thing.

- Some of us have conformed ourselves to the image of an admired preacher or mentor. (Remember the command of our Lord to Peter, "You must follow me!")

- Still others have relied on their heritage, education or even the size of their ministry to make them feel successful.

It could be any number of things, but simply put, they are off the mark.

Walking a New Path

The path is called *Spiritual Formation*.

- Spiritual formation is not a program or a technique that you can bring in the church.

- It is not a one size fits all. It's a life-long process of God working in you as a uniquely created being.

- It is a process of being conformed to the image of Christ for the sake of others. (Romans 8:29)

- It is a desire to know Christ and to be known by Him.

- It is a consuming passion that is fueled by the practice of spiritual disciplines.

Discipline is very unpopular in our culture, yet through the practice of the classic spiritual disciplines we are not bound to prescribed ways of doing things. We are able to participate with God as He works in us. Again Paul wrote:

> "Work out your salvation with fear and trembling, for it is God who works in you to will and to act in order to fulfill his good purpose."
>
> Philippians 2:12–13

Which is it? Do it yourself or let God? In the process of Spiritual formation, it is both.

THE SOIL OF STILLNESS AND SILENCE

"Because we look for the bonfire, we miss the candle.
Because we listen for the shout, we miss the whisper."[3]

Recently I drove to a church to do a consultation. While many of the churches I serve are small in size and remote in location, this one was really out in the boondocks. As I drove from the city to a small town, I took a two lane lightly traveled highway. From there I took a left into one of the several national forests in our state. Several miles of a deserted road led to an even less traveled gravel road then a right and another left. I was convinced I was thirty miles on the other side of the Great Commission when I rounded a bend in the road and there it was, the church I was looking for. I was a little early and it was a cool evening so as I waited on the committee members to arrive, I lowered my windows. It wasn't long until I noticed how very still and quiet it was out there. I have a habit of talking out loud to myself on these trips, so I whispered, "...wow, it's quiet out here." My whisper sounded like a shout! I sat for those few minutes and took in the silence before the first person arrived. (I heard them coming for several miles).

We're Afraid of Stillness and Silence

Unless you live someplace like I just described, you seldom have stillness or silence in your life. Our culture is almost devoid of either of these most important spiritual disciplines. Many of us are afraid of them, and usually do everything we can to avoid them. Almost all of our public worship services have no time for silence. I have preached on these disciplines from time to time and often times I conduct a little experiment. After a short disclaimer, (or warning), I stand still in the pulpit and ask for a time of silence and stillness for sixty seconds. It's not long before nervous giggles break out or someone coughs or yawns. Sometimes people become so uncomfortable that they have to leave the building, breaking the quiet.

Simply put, we just don't like either of these things, yet they are essential to self care and restoration. With all the noise in our lives, many times God's voice gets drowned out.

Where are you God?

Consider what happened to the prophet Elijah and how God spoke to him. He was doing what God had told him to do. He was zealous for the things of God.

He had a big showdown on Mount Carmel with the prophets of Baal, and the Lord won! He killed all the false prophets and the Lord even brought rain as a testimony of His power. That's pretty powerful stuff. But anytime God does something great in the life of His people, somebody's not going to like it. Elijah's *somebody* was King Ahab's wife Jezebel. She sent people out to kill him for all the things he had done. In 1 Kings 19, Elijah has a melt-down. He looks at heaven and says, "I've had it! I'm ready to die! Just take my life!" He lays down exhausted and depressed. After sleeping awhile, the Lord tells him to go stand on the mountain in His presence. Then God did three very powerful things as Elijah watched.

1. A mighty wind tore the mountains apart and shattered the rocks.

2. An earthquake crumbled what was left.

3. A fire scorched the earth.

You would think that Elijah would have shouted and danced and had a fit knowing he was in the presence of the Most High. But God was not in any of these things, as powerful and awesome as they were. In the midst of the stillness and silence that followed was a gentle whisper. It was the voice of God speaking to Elijah as he had always spoken to him. The Lord was calling him back to his side with the gentleness of a shepherd calling a lamb back to the flock.

What about You?

You can probably identify with the prophet.

- You're weary of the work of ministry

- You've thought, "Maybe it's time to get out and get a 'real' job"

- You might be fighting depression or exhaustion with their numerous side effects

- Your spouse and family may seem distant

- You have been busy doing the powerful things of God, yet you seem to be powerless yourself

- You have been asking, *Where are you God?*

The only way to hear God is to drown out everything else. You've got to get to a place of stillness and silence. I used to hate being silent or quiet. I have trouble sitting still. As I'm typing this, my iPod is blasting some song I'm not listening to, so that things won't be so quiet. But let me share something that I've discovered about this.

Stillness and silence is not loneliness, it is time alone with God.

I want lightning and thunder. I want power. I want fire to rain down from heaven. I want my life to be filled with the power of the Holy Spirit. Well, guess what? It won't be until I get still and silent and listen to the whisper that sounds like a SHOUT. God rarely speaks with smoke and fire and crashes of thunder. He's not the, "Great and Powerful Wizard of Oz." He is the all powerful, all knowing, all present Lord that chooses to whisper to your heart.

THE SEED OF SURRENDER

"Going a little farther, he fell to the ground and prayed that if possible the hour might pass from him. "Abba, Father," he said, 'Everything is possible for you. Take this cup from me. Yet not what I will, but what you will'."

Mark 14:35–36

The Prayer that Never Fails

My dad had heart disease for most of his adult life. He had three or four heart attacks that took him to the edge of death and when he was fifty-nine he had heart bypass surgery. At this time, I was in my late thirties and had not really thought much about his mortality, or my own for that matter. When he came out of surgery, he was not doing well; it seems the doctor had forgotten to tell him to stop taking his daily aspirin so he was bleeding uncontrollably. He was rushed back into surgery to check on what was happening and we weren't really sure if he was going to make it. For the first time in my life, my strong dad was faced with possible death. Our family went into a tail-spin. Being the eldest I tried my best to hold our family together. I spent most of the night praying like I had never prayed before. As a pastor I had been through this with several families, but this time it was *my* dad.

As the night progressed, my praying became more and more desperate. I began to bargain with God. You've probably done this at some time in your life. I struggled in my prayer, asking God for just five more years of life for my dad. Finally, exhausted and desperately needing sleep, I prayed the prayer that never fails; "Thy will be done!" I instantly fell asleep having surrendered my earthly father to the loving arms of my Heavenly Father.

My dad had another heart attack that almost took his life and forced him to retire...at seventy-five! He lived another 5 years and passed away at age eighty. While I was asking for 5 years, God had planned twenty-one! I've learned that no matter what the outcome the prayer that never fails is, "Thy will be done".

Sweet Surrender

Gethsemane was a small grove of trees on the Mount of Olives. It was the stage for some of the most agonizing hours in the life of Christ. While His inner circle slept, He poured out His life in prayer to the Father. He asked the Father if He could avoid the cross if at all possible, knowing that it was His ultimate destination. In the final hours of desperate prayer, He sweats drops of blood in his agony. Finally, He prayed, "Thy will be done!" In those four words we find the most important discipline that we can practice: surrender. Stillness and silence lead us to prayer. Prayer ultimately leads us to surrender. Surrender leads us to transformation.

Most of us travel the traditional path of *doing*.

When something happens and our sense of security is threatened, we jump onto the traditional path in search of regaining control. The pattern is as follows:

- We seek information, which we believe will give us a handle on what is happening.

- We seek understanding, believing that if we understand what is going on, we will be able to solve the problem.

- With fresh understanding, we now return to our search for information, only this time it is information that will address the problem.

- Information and understanding in hand, we develop a plan to address the issue and we feel secure again.

- The plan usually gives birth to some kind of program(s).

- When a new program is in place we feel like we are back in control.

We often say, "Things are back under control. We've got our arms around the problem."

Control is so important to us that we often rely on our efforts, programs, plans, ambition, drive, etc. to maintain our felt sense of being in control and secure.

Here's the problem.

1. The traditional path doesn't work. Life changes so fast that by the time we have it figured out, new challenges arise.

2. Control is all about self-enthronement (being in charge which is the essence of sin). Therefore, we are pursuing a path that God cannot honor.

3. Since it is the only path we know we keep working harder and running the treadmill faster.

4. Fatigue/Failure/Conviction/Desperation all eventually lead us to the place of surrender.

Surrender Has Been His Plan and Desire All Along.

We may pray something like this: "Lord Jesus, I (we) can't do it. This is your church, your problem, your people, please come and take over to do whatever you please."

Surrender is the way God works and the path He honors.

It is the cry of Jesus when He was knocking at the door of the church in Revelation 3:20 said, "Let me back in. Quit trying to run the show yourselves."

The following are truths about surrender that every pastor should be reminded of.

- Renewal is possible only after surrender

- Surrender is rewarded with revelation

- The very thing we crave is the reward of surrender

- Surrender leads to fresh wisdom and direction

- Fresh revelation creates true security

- True security is found in a Person, not in plans.

- True security comes when the King of the universe is reigning as the King of your life (and church)

- New or clear direction is born out of revelation

- Programs are valuable, plans and information are essential, but God will never remove our need to live by faith

- He gives us direction. Direction that flows out of the person and fresh work of God gives birth to courage

- Courage is exactly what we need…. It is what our children, grandchildren need to see in us as we follow Christ sacrificially

- Romans 12:1–2, Proverbs 3:5–6, John 5:19–20, John 15

Unfortunately, at every stage in the process there is a temptation to drift. The temptation is to replace the fruit of surrender with the product of control driven effort. Surrender does not come easy, and once given it is easy to drift back into old ways. The temptation is real and unavoidable because wise leaders realize the power of understanding, information, plans, and programs.

While these are things we need and use, they are not the things on which we rely!

Examples to read and consider

The church at Ephesus:
    Driven by the task
    Passion replaced by accomplishment
    Building a great church, organizationally

The church at Laodicea:
    Distracted by the methods
    Passion replaced by activity
    Self-sufficiency will not be tolerated by Jesus.

THE ROOTS OF CALLING

"Foxes have dens and birds have nests, but the Son of Man has no place to lay his head."

Matthew 8:20

I'm sure they thought they knew what they were doing. They had limited knowledge and had not really grasped what was about to happen when Jesus resolutely set out for Jerusalem. Three men, who had been caught up in the excitement of the parade and the idea of the Kingdom, were challenged by our Lord. They had a heart for following. They truly loved the thought of being a Jesus person. They just didn't see what the Lord saw.

One excitedly approached the Master with a declaration. "I will follow you wherever you go!" he proclaimed. Jesus didn't answer like he thought he would. He was expecting a cheerful embrace and an extended hand of inclusion. He got a surprise. Jesus said that though the animals have places of refuge, he did not. He wanted him to look past the protection of the walls of the city and the comfort of the palace to a hill that led to a cross.

Another wanted to follow the Lord, but he wanted to wait until after his father died. This religious and cultural practice was quite acceptable and had become a religious right. Jesus's reply was once again surprising. He said that the dead should bury the dead, but that he should proclaim the Kingdom. The sacrifice for this disciple was to bury the religious and cultural practices that gave him comfort and security. There was nothing necessarily wrong with these things; they were just delaying the calling that was on the follower's life.

The last was possibly the hardest. He wanted to take some time to go back and say goodbye to his family. His sacrifice was his relationships. Jesus responded in what seems to be a harsh rebuke, and once again it was a surprise. How could Jesus ask us to lay our relationships on the altar of the Kingdom? Does our calling really require us to place the plow in the dirt and set our sight on the cross of Calvary? As hard as it might seem, the answer is yes. Every relationship must come second to the Kingdom. That will mean setting your sights on the hill with the cross and plow toward it. He becomes your all in all.

It is time for you to retrace your steps back to your calling. Go back to that time when you knew the Master had come by your life and said, "Follow Me." You may not have heard the voice of God, but through the leadership of the Holy Spirit and the confirmation of the Word and the people of God, you knew he had asked you to commit your life to Christian service. As I speak to pastors and church staff members, I often ask them to share their calling with me. I am amazed at how many can voice their testimony of salvation, but cannot describe when God called them. Some have actually told me that they chose ministry as a profession. Much like one chooses to be a lawyer or doctor or some other professional, they chose to go into the work of ministry. I am equally astonished by the numbers of those individuals who have crumbled under the weight of the many trials and tribulations that come about because of the stress of ministry. Simply put, you must rely on the call of God upon your life in order to sustain yourself in ministry. If you can do anything else besides be in ministry, DO IT! But if you know that God has called you to serve in his Kingdom, for all of our sakes don't run from it.

How can you know that God has called you?

1. You have a passion to lead and serve God's people.

2. This service brings you joy; it is the reason you get up in the morning.

3. It is not a job, it's your life!

4. You know the time in your life when Jesus called you to be a leader in His kingdom.

But be sure of this; following God's call will cost you. As the three would-be followers of Christ found out, the call of Christ will require that he is first before every other aspect of your life. That includes family, home and all the other things we hold dear. So many are called to places too far, too hard or too costly in their estimation. Because of this, they follow the Master on their own terms. That simply will not do. You must follow Christ no matter where He leads. He may be leading you down the street from your grandchildren. If so, follow Him. He may be leading you to places unknown. Again, follow Him.

Remember this old hymn?

It may be through the shadows dim, or ore the stormy sea.

I'll take my cross and follow Him, wherever he leadeth me.

Wherever he leads I'll go, wherever he leads I'll go.

I'll follow my Christ who loves me so; wherever he leads I'll go![4]

THE BRANCHES OF ADORATION

"Then he said to Thomas, 'Put your finger here; see my hands. Reach out your hand and put it into my side. Stop doubting and believe.'

Thomas said to him, 'My Lord and my God!'"

John 20:27–28

It had been a nightmarish week. The man he had placed all his hopes in had died. It was not an ordinary death, it was a spectacle. The mockery of a trial before the Roman authorities, the scourging and beating until he was unrecognizable, the parade of criminals, and finally the crucifixion was just too much for him to bear. He had always been a practical man. He was one of those "if the shoe fits" sort of guys. His closest friends continued to hide fearing they would meet with the same fate as their master. Then they claimed to have had seen him. Jesus was alive and doing quite well. He refused to believe it. Maybe it was the hurt or the disappointment, but he could not bear to go down that path again.

They talked him in to meeting with them in their place of hiding. The hope was that Jesus would come to them again and that Thomas would finally see for himself. As the gathering continued, he appeared. "Peace be with you," Jesus said, and then he turned his attention to the doubting one. "Come here and see for yourself." Jesus lovingly said. Thomas fell before Jesus and worshipped him. His proclamation was clear and to the point, "My Lord and my God!" It was authentic worship.

Just mention the word worship in any church these days and it won't be long before an argument breaks out.

- We argue about what songs to sing to Him.

- Should we sing the words while looking at a hymnal or from a screen? Let's not get anyone upset so let's do both.

- In one service we sing one hundred year old hymns accompanied by the piano and organ. In another we sing songs written in the last twenty years and accompanied by guitars and drums. Sometimes we blend the two together.

- Southern Gospel and Country twang is the genre of choice in some churches; Beethoven and Bach are highly regarded in others. All the while, we have missed the point.

The essential nature of worship can be found in a practical, disheartened man realizing he had come face to face with God in the flesh. In four words he describes the heart of worship; Adoration. The Scripture doesn't say so, but I imagine him falling to his knees, forehead on the nail pierced feet as he made his declaration. Notice three principles that this encounter teaches.

1. You can practice any style of worship you desire and not really worship. That's because it's not about the style, it's about the heart.

2. Authentic worship comes from a relationship with God.

3. Adoration is directed toward God and is all about God.

As Pastor/Leaders we must learn to adore God in such a way that when we lead worship it comes from a heart filled with love for God and His people. That cannot just happen on Sunday when we are in the position of leadership. It must happen daily as we practice the disciplines of stillness, silence and surrender.

Early in my ministry I struggled with leading worship. It seemed I always felt unprepared as I stood before God's people. I had studied the text and believed I had a fresh word each Sunday. I thought I was capable. After all, I had been to seminary and knew how to exegete the Scriptures. But something was missing. One Monday, I went to the associational pastor's conference in downtown Oklahoma City. On the way back from lunch I had a talk with Harvey Albright, a much admired pastor in my home town. He was nearing retirement having been pastor of his church for over 30 years. We began talking about how he was known for making hundreds of visits. He would visit people in the hospitals, at their place of work and in their homes. When he could find people at home, he would go door to door sharing the Gospel. I asked him how he was able to do that and his reply surprised me. After some silence he said, "You know, Monty, if I had it to do all over again, I'd spend less time visiting and more time alone with the Father. You need to remember that." That statement revolutionized my ministry. More time with the Father, worshipping and adoring Him. If something's missing… maybe you've found it.

THE LEAVES OF ENDURANCE

"For we wrestle not against flesh and blood, but against the principalities, against the powers, against the rulers of the darkness of this world, against spiritual wickedness in high places."

Ephesians 6:12

I have always been intrigued with the Civil War. I am a great-great grandson of a Confederate veteran. Grandpa Rufus ran off from his adoptive parents when he was fourteen and joined up with the Texas Cavalry during the Red River campaign. As a full blooded Cherokee he had grown up in the woods of Eastern Tennessee. He was great with a rifle, small in stature and an excellent tree climber. So, they made him a sniper. In one battle a Yankee mini ball took out his left eye exiting his head very near his left ear. He fell out of the tree and nearly died on the battlefield that day. He bore the scars and the frequent headaches for the rest of his life.

You can probably identify with Rufus. You surrendered to the ministry. You have found yourself on the front lines using your strengths and talents. Maybe you have been wounded, left for dead, and now carry the scars and pain in your spiritual body. The apostle Paul described our struggle as "...not against flesh and blood, but against the rulers, against the authorities, against the powers of this dark world…" It is a battle, literally for the souls of men, and the result will be Heaven or Hell. It takes great courage and tremendous strength to stay engaged in this battle. Doubtless, there has been at least one time that you wanted to quit. Some of you want to quit right now. Well, let me share two other things about ole Grandpa Rufus.

1. He didn't quit because he was wounded. He continued to fight. He carried his pain and his wounds back into subsequent battles. His passion overcame his pain.

2. He never got any credit for his service. Because he was so young when he joined the confederate army, they never officially signed him up. As a result he never won a medal. There is no official record of his service. It's as if it never happened, but it certainly did. Rufus knew it did, and he had the extra hole in his head to prove it.

If you are going to be in the battle, those two things must be part of your value system. Your passion must overcome your pain, and it does not matter whether or not you get credit for your service. You must fight on for the cause of Christ. As a pastor, you are a hero of the

Kingdom. The most admired of our country's heroes are those who humbly did their duty for the cause.

Reid Pepper

Reid Pepper was such a hero. When I met him I didn't know what he had done for our country. He was a member of my church, recently widowed and a very friendly guy. Every so often he would come by my office to visit during the day. He seemed like he was in need of a friend, and quickly became mine. During one of our short conversations I asked him if he was in World War II. His reply was interesting, "Yes I served with some great guys." "What was your rank?" I inquired. "Sergeant" was his proud reply. "Really?" I said. "Sergeant Pepper!" I said jokingly. "That's right." His wide smile quickly turned to an all out laugh.

Reid came by several times. We'd drink some coffee, he would reminisce about days gone by, and then he would be on his way. I really didn't think much of the visits. Just an old guy needing a friend, I thought. Then one night I watched *"Saving Private Ryan"* the movie about a group of soldiers in World War II looking for the only surviving son of a family. I was moved by the horror of the war as depicted by Tom Hanks and Steven Spielberg. The next Sunday I saw Reid. I quickly thrust out my hand and said, "Sergeant Pepper, I just want to thank you for what you did for me in the war!" "What's got into you Preacher?" he replied. "Well, I watched *Saving Private Ryan* the other day. Have you seen it?" I asked. "No, and I don't plan to!" he snapped back, "I guess I don't want to relive all that."

The next week he came by the office. He had his head down as we began to talk. He apologized for being so gruff with me the Sunday before. "It's still very raw, even after all these years," he said as tears began to well up in his eyes. Then he began to tell me about how he and several of his buddies found themselves in Belgium and France during the winter of 1944–1945. That's right, the Battle of the Bulge. He shared all the details of how one by one most of the men in his platoon were killed in horrific fashion. He himself was wounded and yet was able to get back to the front lines after several brief stays in a relief station. His stories moved me. We wept together as he told me of losing a close friend that had entered the war with him. I cried when he told me of the victory he experienced as his unit bravely ran into machine gun fire and broke through the enemy lines. He held back some of the more graphic details of which I am grateful.

As I sat there I realized that I was visiting with a real hero. He wasn't a movie star play acting through a series of scenes then retreating to the comfort of his multi-million dollar mansion. He was the real deal. He received some medals and was welcomed home by a grateful nation, but now he was just an old guy sitting in a pastor's office in a small town sharing his stories. Sergeant Reid Pepper did his duty and because of his willingness to die for freedom, you and I are free today.

Every week I talk to pastors like you in my office, on the telephone and through email. I listen to your stories. Sometimes we cry together as you tell of the losses you have experienced in your life. Other times we celebrate as you share your victories. Through it all I've come to realize that I get to sit and visit with heroes. Not just heroes of some foreign war, but heroes of the eternal Kingdom of the living God. Most of us serve in out of the way places and live in humble surroundings, but remember this; there is a crown of righteousness waiting in heaven for those who endure. So, endure my friend, endure!

THE FRUIT OF JOY

"The thief comes only to steal and kill and destroy; I have come that they may have life, and have it to the full."

John 10:10

When my wife and I were in our late '20s, we went to the airport to have a baby. Yes, that's right the airport. While all the other couples we knew had made that edge-of-your-seat ride to the local hospital, we dressed in our Sunday best, excitedly got in our little car and drove to the airport. Back then you could go to the gate where the airplane was arriving to wait on your expected loved ones we stood there for what seemed like hours. Finally, the *silver stork* carrying our precious child arrived. Her escort was the last to get off. Instead of hustling off to their rental cars and baggage claim, every passenger including the crew waited as the big moment arrived. Our case worker got off the plane and down the chute she came with our baby girl. As she was placed in her momma's arms the entire crowd burst into joyful applause. From that moment we fell in love and she is the joy of our life.

Every time I relive that moment a smile comes to my face (I'm smiling now as I write this). Joy invades my life. Not because our daughter is still a baby fresh off the airplane from South Korea, but because she has grown up to be a beautiful young woman. I have seven photos of her in my office. I have two others that I keep in my wallet, ready to show at a moment's notice. My joy has continued to grow since that day in 1983 when she came down that chute.

Our Lord declares that He has come to give us abundant life. I used to think that was a one-time event. Give your life to Christ, experience the joyful applause of other Christians and that was it. However, I now know that Christ gives us abundant life as we go through it with Him. Not all the days will be good days. Some will be frustrating and hard; some will be sad and lonely; still others will be joyful. Some read the declaration of Jesus and think about temporal things like food, clothes, houses and big bank accounts. Things they already have, yet long for more. Their question is, "When does this abundant life thing kick in?"

It all has to do with passion. Some folks have a passion for hunting, so when they're hunting, they are joyfully living the abundant life. Others have a passion for the weekends, so when the weekend comes around you can't keep them from smiling. Still others have a passion for ministry so they spend their lives ministering.

If you have a passion for Jesus Christ, you will have what He came to give you, abundant life. There will be photos of Him all over your heart. You'll be ready to show them when others ask about Him. He will be your joy no matter what life brings you. That is living life abundantly.

What's happened to our joy? Many times when I go to church, be it my own or one that I am preaching or consulting at, I don't see a lot of joy. The general consensus is that life is terrible and it comes out in different ways. You've heard them.

- Well, I'm here
- Things are okay under the circumstances
- You keep this sanctuary too cold
- That music is _____a. too loud. b. too slow. c. terrible

On and on it goes. I'm talking about church members who feel they have a right to a life free of worry and distress. Now, we all have tough times. Jesus never promised any of us that we would lead a care-free life filled with one happy day after another. In fact, He guaranteed that in this world we would have trouble. That's a statement of fact. But He also guaranteed, "I have overcome the world." So when He says He came to give the abundant life, do you believe it? When the world has overcome you, He says I have overcome the world.

A Lifelong Journey

You may now be thinking, well that was a simple little book. All I have to do is follow this formula and I will thrive in ministry. That is not the intent of this book. In fact, while I have shared some of the struggles and blessings of being in ministry throughout these pages, you and I will never find our perfect stream. This is a lifelong journey of stumbling in and out of the desert and back to the stream.

Like you, I have gone through many desert wanderings in my life. A few years back as I was wandering in the wilderness, a good friend gave me this encouragement:

"Walking around in the wilderness is never fun, but it sure does make us long for the stream..."

He was right. All of the conditions of the desert provoke our desire for God. They beat on us, discourage us and take their toll on our bodies, but they also push us toward the life giving stream. The more of these experiences I go through the tougher they get and the more they push me toward the stream.

So, it's a lifelong journey. We have a God who longs to be with us. He allows us to experience the desert. There He speaks to us about the things that are most important. Through a thankful heart and a contrite spirit we will find our way back to Him.

Keep looking up!

ENDNOTES

1   Thelma Wells, *God give me Victory over Anger*, (Eugene, Oregon: Harvest House Publishers, 2011), 99.

2   Girmchew, The Ethiopian Herald, "General truth about dehydration." Last modified February 25, 2014. Accessed February 25, 2014. www.ethpress.gov.et

3   Max Lucado, *In the Eye of the Storm*, (Nashville, Tennessee: Thomas Nelson, 1991), 91.

4   "Wherever He Leads I'll Go" (no. 437) in *Baptist Hymnal* (Nashville, Tennessee; Lifeway Worship, 2008).

BIBLIOGRAPHY

Benson, Bob, and Michael Benson. *Disciplines for the Inner Life*. Hendersonville, Tennessee: Deeper Life Ministries, 1989.

Blackaby, Henry T., and Richard Blackaby. *Spiritual Leadership*. Nashville, Tennessee: B & H Publishing, 2011.

Blanchard, Ken, and Phil Hodges. *Lead like Jesus*. Nashville, Tennessee: Thomas Nelson, 2005.

Buchanan, Mark. *The Rest of God*. Nashville, Tennessee: Thomas Nelson Inc., 2006.

Burns, Bob, Tasha D. Chapman, and Donald Guthrie. *Resilient Ministry*. Dowers Grove, Illinois: InterVarsity Press, 2013.

Dunn, Ronald. *When Heaven is Silent*. Nashville, Tennessee: Thomas Nelson, 1994.

George, Denise. *What Pastors Wish Church Members Knew.* Grand Rapids, Michigan: Zondervan 2009.

Hart, Archibald D. *Coping with Depression in the Ministry and Other Helping Professions.* Waco, Texas: Word Publishing, 1984.

Iorg, Jeff. *Seasons of a Leaders Life.* Nashville, Tennessee: B & H Publishing, 2013.

Kinnaman, Gary D., and Alfred H. Ells. *Leaders that Last.* Grand Rapids, Michigan: Baker Books, 2003.

London, H.B., and Neil B. Wiseman. *Pastors at Greater Risk.* Ventura, California: Regal Books, 2003.

London, H.B., and Neil B. Wiseman. *They Call me Pastor.* Ventura, California: Regal Books, 2000.

MacDonald, Gordon. *Building Below the Waterline.* Peabody, Massachusetts: Hendrickson Publishing Marketing, 2011.

MacDonald, Gordon. *Going Deep.* Nashville, Tennessee: Thomas Nelson, 2011.

McNeal, Reggie. *A Work of Heart.* San Francisco, California: Jossey-Bass, 2000.

McNeal, Reggie. *Get a Life!.* Nashville, Tennessee: B & H Publishing, 2007.

McNeal, Reggie. *Practicing Greatness.* San Francisco, California: Jossey-Bass, 2006.

Minirth, Frank, Don Hawkins, Paul Meier, and Chris Thurman. *Before Burnout*. Chicago, Illinois: Moody Press, 1990.

Rohrer, David. *The Sacred Wilderness of Pastoral Ministty*. Downers Grove Ill: InterVarsity Press, 2012.

Swenson, Richard A. *Margin*. Colorado Springs, Colorado: NavPress, 2004.

Witt, Lance. *Replenish*. Grand Rapids, Michigan: Baker Books, 2011.